INTERPRETATIONS OF ROMANCE

INTERPRETATIONS OF ROMANCE

Poems that Talk to Humble Hearts

Joseph P. Policape

To order additional copies of this book, contact:
Xlibris Corporation
1-888-795-4274
www.Xlibris.com
Orders@Xlibris.com
32219

ACKNOWLEDGEMENTS

Special thanks to Junior DelaCruz my photographer, and to my special colleagues Jocelyn Joseph and Walson Thomas for their encouragement and good advice.

CONTENTS

BABY, YOU SET ME FREE

Baby, darling, comes to me!
You are my ideal.
The only girl that I love,
Come to me I will make you cheer,
I feel warm at your presence.
Baby, my dear,
The closer you come,
The better I feel.

You are my heartbeat.
I love you, baby, my dear,
Have a little dance with me,
Sit and play with me,
Sit and talk to me,
You make me cheer,
Every time you touch me,
Your presence is like a breeze.

Baby, you excite me.
To you I veiled my secret.
Baby! Oh you're real!
Baby! My darling,
You're my sweetheart.
Come here, darling!
Only in your presence I feel free.

SUCCESS, PASS BY ME

O' success! Ah! Come here!
Come to say hello to me!
I've seen you hiking on my street every day,
But you forget to pass by me.
Come, my dear, I have something to say.

Approach me with your lamenting red
Lips and create jealousy in failure, come near me.
Lie down on my bed.
O' my dear success, come to set me free.
You're welcome with your beautiful red
Lips, my dear success, come to set me free.

Sit in my living room.
Walk with me to the music hall.
I want to be your groom.
Come to me, darling, I will give you all
My heart and I will give you all
My love as long as I am your groom.

You're a ravishing girl forever.
Your lips like Cinderella's and you are fun.
And I love you more than ever.
Put your hand around my shoulder,
Once failure sees you, she will run.
And you will be my love forever.

IF EVER I LOVE YOU

My heart searches for you at morn
My heart searches for you at noon.
You're a groom.
And you are fine looking just like the moon.
Yeah! You are more comely and beauteous than the moon.
Why can't I love you!

My wish that you'll be mine
And that keeps me alive,
As I think of your white teeth in my mind,
They are whiter than snow, and I want to survive.
Your blue eyes make me want to be your groom.
Nothing can make me feel more alive
Than when I think of you as a groom.

My heart searches for you late at night.
You love me and I love you evermore.
You're a groom in my sight,
But it is not a reason for me not to love you more.
When I think of you I can't sleep at night.
There is no one in nature that I can love so much more,
You are so precious, how would I live without you in my sight?

My eyes can't close at night
When I am in the dark room thinking of you.
My heart searches for you late at night.
The love we share is great to me and to you too.
Every night you appear in my dream,
I saw you like the angel Gabriel in the dream.
And if ever I love you,
Nature contrived you for me and you are my only dream.

TRUE LOVE

Unreasoning, they talked about you,
They are too young to understand a clue
about you, and me too,
Until I had a passion to find you.
And I went looking for you.
Then I learned that true love takes two.

When by the beach lay you and me,
I found you have a distinctive charm.
I realized you're real in me,
When you held me in your arm
I didn't apprehend love, I could not see.
And this is one reason many got harmed.

Many of my friends become alarmed.
They are aware that true love takes two.
Those that lack true love injure and harm
True love is just like you and me as we lay in the beach.
I am embarrassing you and you are touching me too.
In loving relationships mutual respect we must reach.

THE ONE WITH THE MAGNIFICENT EYES

The one with the magnificent eyes
Is the only one I love.
I hear your voice come to me as a prize.
I see the one to be my lover is coming like a dove.
I said, here comes my beloved! I arise.
When I saw you, you were like an angel from the skies.

You're my calories in the winter,
You're my ventilation in the summertime.
You sound sweeter than a love letter from the printer.
My blood vibrates when I see the sublime.
"Here is the one with the magnificent eyes," I said.
"They are not blue, gray, black, or red."

"Let me be closer to you," I said.
Warm me with you magnificent eyes.
They are not blue, gray, black, or red.
I pray to God and the angels for my prize.
To make me closer to those beautiful eyes.
Those that are not blue, gray, black, or red.

BY THE BEACH

We went by the sea.
I sat on the sand with my lover.
Then I went to my knee.
I thank God for my darling, the one that I discover.
My lover pinched me as we walk in the sand.
We plunged into the water, everyone could see.
Deeper, deeper in the sea we went as I kissed her hand.
We swam in the mist of the current, as I said, "I love thee."
As the wind blew in the sky
The rain fell, and nature came to testify,
That love exists under the sky.

Darling, dance with me,
You are the pupil of my eyes.
Hold me tight, oh I plead!
We are free under the sky.
Do not fear the current, my dear.
You're with me, none to fear
I will take you to shore, you will see.
Nature will come to testify that we
are in love, you and me.

Darling, roll in the sand with me,
Embrace me, touch me, and squeeze me.
Let us go deeper, deeper into the sea,
As tornadoes rumble above, touch me.
Let us go deeper, deeper into the sea,
There is nothing to fear for you and me.
We are together and we are in love.

WHY I LOOK AT YOU IN THE EYE

I have been looking at you in the eye?
I want to tell you that I love you,
But I am shy.
I am afraid you won't love me too.
So I sigh
Every time I see you,
And my eyes went to the sky,
I pray for that wonder to betide.

Come, darling, to tell me you love me,
Say you love me, I promise once again
I'll love you when you're sick, count on me.
To love you even if you're blind, you will see.
Or even if you are without teeth.
We'll always share each other's pain.

I don't know why
You can't tell me you do.
Just look at me in the eye,
You will never lie.

Oh! It will be a festival,
When you and I will lie,
When you and I in love.
Oh! Help me, God, I pray!
In the middle of the night,
You and I will wake up to play,
I will tell you why,
When we obtain love.
I used to look at you in the eye.

WHY DO I LOVE DENISE

I love Denise,
By virtue of her love for me,
In time of calamity,
In time of peace
Or anguish, she is always nice.

I love Denise,
She was ordained before my birth.
She loves me in time of famish.
She stayed with me when I was near death.
I was sick, she stuck with me and she was nice.

I love Denise because she's nice.
She cares for me.
Whenever I am in trouble, I called Denise.
By virtue of her love for me, my soul finds peace.
Oh my dear Denise, you are always nice.

SPRING

Here is spring!
Let's plant seeds.
My sweet posy will spring up while we sing.
Come on, my sweetheart, let's cut the weeds.
Send winter back to its pit.
I can walk in my parterre to watch my good deeds.
O darling, while we watch them grow, let's sit.
I've been waiting for you sweet,
To send my dear children to play,
Play with you like a toy while the children eat.
Yea! Play on the grass in May,
I see my buds open up, oh how neat.
And I feel spring in my soul, my head, and feet.

You have finally showed up
My little flowers can spring up!
They are red, green, and violet—how sweet.
Yeah, play with my little pup
My beautiful garden can grow up
My children can now play, while I sit.

Send winter away, lovely spring.
In my little garden I will sit.
To watch my buds open up while I sing.
They are red, green, and violet—how sweet.
Come, my sweet spring,
Send winter back to its pit.

THE FOOLISH LOVE

Like the sea, why is love so frail? It makes me feel belittled.
The wave of love, like the ocean, is deep and resilient.
Swimming in violent sea makes one very little.
As a novice captain I refused to ride a boat in water that's violent.
So like the violent sea, living with a woman that is violent makes me feel belittled.

Like the temperature, my life is gloomy,
My way is a pitfall.
My tenderness is feathered away with worry,
Like plants in dry land its branches evaporate and fall,
So my commitment to a violent woman will not tarry.

I am willing to suffer so my ally can live with joy,
But the heart of the woman is like a stone,
She can't endure affliction and treat her partner as a boy.
Like an inexperienced captain in a violent sea, my love is a foolish one,
For living with a woman such as her is a phenomenon.

As a sinking boat, my love for her is gone.
But I go deeper and deeper in the stream of love
But our relationship is about to sink, but the captain is holding on.
Our relationship won't survive even with the help of the gods above.
I won't stay in a relationship that is getting more brutal, it is wrong.

LIVING TOGETHER

Darling, we are living together.
It shall be a great adventure for me and for you.
If love is abiding, our children shall be happy.
We shall make each other cheer.
I shall love you; you shall love me too.
And with me you shall never be unhappy.

Let's put God first, and our posterity shall have peace.
The kin shall arise with virtue.
I love you and I will do my best to make you merry
When the Holy Ghost lives in us everything shall be nice.
We shall have authority over the spirit of voodoo.
Living together shall be as sweet as cherry.

I shall make sacrifice to satisfy you.
I want to be the one to know about your troubles.
We will admire each other for life.
You shall want to make sacrifice for your family too.
If we really love, our blessing from above shall be doubled.
You are a wonderful wife.

We are now carrying the same name.
We are no longer strangers to each other.
We became one flesh and blood.
Our thinking will always be the same.
I love you, darling, just like my mother.
Darling, if we are faithful, God will raise us from the mud.

I owe you all my love.
You owe me all your love.
My soul shall never mind elsewhere.
I don't expect your spirit to mind elsewhere.
We shall live like doves.
Your presence to me scented likes myrrh,
Our love just starts.
It begins in the heart.

On Saturday, August 23, 1986

MARRIAGE IN THE 21ST CENTURY

A decision to marry in the 21st century might be a foolish one.
You just start your own misery and division.
Virtuous women are hard to find and earnest men are rare.
To find a good partner, you should always be in prayer.

If you are able find a good partner, hold him or her tight, especially one who wants to share.
So many are not too kind, and toward men the court is not too fair.
O, man! Enjoy each day you sleep at your own home, I swear.
Once she begins to call you lazy, always carry a shirt in your car to wear.

Why creating your own woe,
Marriage today is an addition of all problems, so go slow.
If you are willing to get married, be ready to sleep in snow.
It is a multiplication to our miseries that will grow.

Marriage is a subtraction of all liberties and a probable division.
Before you're marrying, envision,
You will divorce with the scorn and it won't be your decision.
All your savings will be gone in addition.

All is because of your compulsion to marry
Now you are living with a broken heart.
Don't marry; you will live longer and you won't feel scary.
These days, a man must be smart.

Marry if you wish and never live in peace again.
Restraining orders are without borders.
Make a choice, my dear friend, you have a brain.
With restraining orders you won't be free, they are government orders.

A LITTLE CURSE

When I first met her, we sat alone in the breeze.
It was calm and peaceful for the entire time.
With her love I was pleased.
We began to speak about love for the first time.
We started a new chapter in life.
It was like music with a perfect rhyme.
I could feel that she was going to be my wife.
I did not know how amoral she was at that time.

She gave me hope and I gave her hope.
She became my lover, a woman that my heart desired.
The way we met it looked like it was our scope.
I became her lover, and for her I was inspired.
She made me believe in her,
And for her I was really inspired.
But it was my destruction that I was working for.

Or I would never have loved a woman.
Now I never regretted it for my kin.
I still believe that I was born to be her man.
Meeting her was also a sin.
And I regretted the day she and I met.
I will always be part of her because of our kin.
As the saying says, "What you see is what you get!"
But I still believe our meeting was a sin.

I don't hate her and I'll never hate her,
She was the first woman that I ever fell in love with,
But whenever I think of her, I see blur.
She is the last woman that I'll ever fall in love with.
Each time I see my kin,
I remember the day we sat together, August fifth.
But our encounter was a curse and sin.

YOU'RE NOT EDITH BU MY CURSE

I had a dream.
I saw a beautiful woman.
When she saw me she hid behind a tree.
She looked just like Edith,
The woman that God planned to give me,
The woman chosen by my parent
The woman whose parents loved me,
Edith was my parent's only plea.

She came and gave me a kiss.
I said, you're a curse, not Edith!
You're not Edith, Miss!
I'd never fall in love with you.
You're not Edith!
You're not Edith from start.
Why should I ever marry you?
If I fall in love with you, you'll break my heart.
I pushed her away.

In the dream, she pulled me.
She looked like she shone.
She gave me a soft caress
She put her mouth on mine.
I obeyed her,
And said to her, let's go dine!

It wasn't long after I met her
She asked me to go for a glass of wine.
"I'm a Nazarene, I don't drink," I said.
The dream had come true.
She put her mouth on mine.
She put me to sleep just like a baby on her lap.
She gave me some wine
I went into a nap.

I'M FREE ALL OF A SUDDEN

I was looking for a friend when you came on my way,
And you brought me joy every day.
You brought me love and happiness.
You took away all my sadness.
You brought me joy and perfect peace.
Oh darling, you're nice.

Just like Adam in Eden,
I'm free all of a sudden!
I am happy with you only.
I'm no longer lonely.
Just like Adam in Eden,
I'm free all of a sudden.
I found a mate that I love,
Darling, I feel like a dove

You and I are inseparable,
Because you're incomparable.
I promise to love and cherish you.
You promise to love me too.
I have no doubt of your love for me.
Oh darling, you set me free.
God will bring blessing upon us,
God will bring us peace plus.

Just like Adam in Eden,
I'm free of all a sudden!
I am happy with you only.
I'm no longer lonely.
Just like Adam in Eden,
I'm free all of a sudden.
I found a mate to love,
And I am love.

ONE HEART

You and I are united in love,
Forever with one heart.
We will keep our pledge and live like doves.
And nothing will keep us apart.
For the invisible God is in our vows.

It was a dream when you approached me.
You said to me that you loved me.
It was a dream when I said to you that I cherished you.
Oh dear, God sent you on my way to set me free.
Today we make a vow to walk always hand in hand.

I love it when you look in my eyes.
It means that you love me always and forever.
It was true when you said you love me with all your heart.
And darling, I love you more than ever.
It was true that for me God has set you apart.

Forever, darling, you and I are united in love.
Forever, darling, we will always love and cherish each other.
Help us we pray, oh God, to keep our vows and live like doves.
Till death and forever!

WE PLAYED

Since I met you, we have been played.
We've not been playing the guitar,
We've not been playing the drum, or the clarinet,
But we played hide-and-seek under the shade.

We played in the morning,
We played in the afternoon,
We played in the evening,
We were never scared of any warning.

We played under the corn trees,
We played on the pistachios, and we're not innocents
We played in the fields, and at home behind our parents.
We played and squeezed.

We played in the morning,
We played in the afternoon,
We played in the evening,
We played without fear of warning.

Then your mother asked, "What happen to you?
How did your stomach become so big?
Did you disobey my view?
I do not think you would have been played with that boy!
I can't picture these types of scenes of you lying.
Tell me if you thought the boy thing was a toy."

Sorry, Mother, we have been playing.
We played in the morning,
We played in the afternoon,
We played in the evening,
We played without warning.

Yes, Mother, sometimes we go with the breeze.
We played under the banana trees,
We had to play under the bamboo trees and squeeze,
We played as we watched the chugging bee.

Mama, you warned me of the danger of playing with the boy.
I played in the morning, afternoon, and evening.
You told me the boy's thing was not a toy.
But I played with it and forgot your warning.
Now it is too late for me to learn that the boy's thing was not a toy.

YOU'RE EVERYTHING TO ME

You're everything to me,
You're the only one I see,
God shaped you for me.
What a joy to know
You'll be there even when it snows.
We have the same view,
And you love me too.
What a joy to find you!
Before my God I bow,
And made a vow
To always love you.

Oh how perfect to find a true mate!
One who's always great!
It's like God created you for me in this globe.
You're the one who bought me my nicest robe.
You are the one that I will always admire.
I love to hear you play the lyre.

I love you more than the sun.
Darling, you are fun.
I love you more than the rain.
When I am with you, I have no pain.
Everything we do together is in unity.
You are one who's full of dignity.
You're everything to me,
You're the one that set me free.

EDITH MY BEAUTIFUL

NATHANAEL

Good morning, my Beautiful Edith!
How do you do?
The sunrises in my heart when I see you,
Your presence fills me like dew.

EDITH

I am fine.
Thank you for your compliment,
But don't let Mama hear you,
She won't be glad.
You understand me!
Don't let Mama hear you.
She'll be mad.

NATHANAEL

I've seen you go by each morning
Ere the sunrises, while
The dew is still on the roses.
I love your smile.
You're carrying the bucket beautifully.
Why are you awake so early?

EDITH

Sir, I'm gonna draw water for my mama.
She's poor and busy working to raise us.
I always wake up early to practice my drama,
And my little sisters, brothers are young and plus
My mother has to provide all our substances.
I wake up early daily to bring water to the house, sir,
And that's my way to support her.

NATHANAEL

You're doing well, darling!
If I tell you that
You're an intelligent woman,
Don't be alarmed.
I can see your external beauty,
But I can sense your inner charm.

NATHANAEL

Let me help you carry the bucket.
The road is beautiful,
The sun hasn't risen yet.
It is cool.
The dew is not beginning to fall yet.
We can have some dialogues,
About making a pledge to each other.

EDITH

Sir, what are you saying to me?
What is a pledge?
We're children, please; please, sir!
You know the people in this town.
They say things they don't see.
Ultimately, they'll whisper,
If you give them a chance.
If you need to talk,
Please go talk to my mother.

NATHANAEL

You're my dream come true, darling.
You're beautiful and wise.
I've dreamt about you ere we even met.
Please look at me in the eyes,
Say to me you love me.

EDITH

Please, sir,
Don't get me in trouble.
I am not ready for romance
I have a poor family
My mother counts on me
My little sisters and brothers count on me
My teachers trust me.
I must preserve my dignity.
If you have anything to say to me,
Please go see my mother.

EDITH

And
Sir, I am sure that you love me,
But if you really care about me,
Wait until I grow up.
I'll realize my education,
I'll learn how to love from my teachers.

NATHANAEL

Miss, you have intelligence,
Gee! You look like a dove!
Don't repeat the mistake of our grandparents,
Who were afraid to speak about love.
I can be you best teacher,
To teach you about real romance.

NATHANAEL

I know you care for your family, but
You can have affection for someone,
And still help your siblings and little pup.
You can be in love and still assist Mama.
You can be attracted to a guy,
While you are growing up,
You can be in love, and trust yourself.

NATHANAEL

Love is not sex.
Someone who really loves you
Will not ask you for sex before marriage
Can you please talk to me?
I love you, Edith!
Edith, Edith, I love you!
You're all I need to tell me you do.

EDITH

Monsieur, oh!
I know you love me
I love you too,
When we are ready we will conjugate the verb of love.
Please, please, sir, let me go!
Let me go before the people in this town,
Complain to my mama.

NATHANAEL

Trust me, darling,
I'll be your lover,
I'll be your friend,
I'll be your brother,
I'll be a teacher and
A father to you and
For me you'll be a mother.
Put your arm around me,
This is the time
To make our lives complete.

NATHANAEL

Don't run, darling!
I'm not going eat you.
If you run, you might be falling.
I'm not an officer,
I'll not arrest you,
Neither a pleasanter,
I love you forever.

EDITH

Mama, I met a man,
He looks like Angel Gabriel.
Don't look at me so angrily!
He's a handsome man named Nathaniel.
He made me feel happily.

MOTHER

Edith, I told you, away from a man,
He's the most evil creator on this earth.
He can make your mouth bitter.
He can give you morning sickness.
If he takes your virtue,
No doctor on earth can repair it.
A man can damage your
Your stomach for nine months and
People would think you've been poisoned.

EDITH

Mama, I met him by the river of Providence.
Last night I saw him in my revelation.
Everything he said made common sense.
I can hear love like in his salutation.
Honesty in everything he said.

EDITH

Mama, don't cry too loudly.
Don't mention his name Nathanael.
He's sincere and won't violate
My conscience and he's the son of Marie.
He's from a family who's lofty and proudly.

MOTHER

How do you know he really loves you?
Even if he wept, swear, and tear.
How do you know he meant it?
Men can bring tears to their eyes,
They can swear by the heavens and the earth,
That doesn't mean a man is not a liar.

FATHER

If she met him by the river of Providence,
He's not a liar and might be the son of Daniel.
If he swore to her by the tornadoes
He might be the son of Ougou Feray and a liar.
If he wrote a love letter to her,
He might be a man of confidence.
If he swore to her by God, he's Angel Gabriel.

FATHER AND MOTHER

She said he swore to her by God
Oh God of Providence!
We come to you with tremblement,
We ask that you show us evidence
If this man has your temperament
And can he take responsibilities.

TOGETHER

We all heard him calling out that is the evidence.
He's neither an immature nor a fool.
He stands by the gates singing the song of love.
He's a man from God's Providence.
A man of wisdom is more precious than gold,
For God is in everything he does.

PASTOR

We are gathered together
Before God almighty and you, witnesses
To joint together a husband and wife
To you, man, comfort her, honor in sickness
And forsake all other woman.
To you woman, love him, forsake all other men.
As long as you do this you shall live.

CHORUS

Oh how heavenly, what bliss!
When a man and a woman join together,
In marriage to form a unity
May the heaven above bring joy and peace
To their lives and bless
Their home and may their children find comfort.

I PROMISE

When I first met you, I promised to always love you.
I promised to love and be closer to you each and every day.
I promised to always sleep by your side.
I promised when you're with me, you will feel like to play.

I promised to be faithful.
I promised I'll cherish you,
I promised to bring joy to your heart,
I promised to always stick by your side like glue.

I promised for my thoughts to be yours,
I promised you'll be my lover and best friend.
I promised to carry you when you can't walk.
I promised to never let you alone with the chores.

I promised to be tender and kind.
I promised to give you all my love.
I promised to cross with you the highest tide.
I promised I'll climb the highest mountain for you.
I promised to be your man,
Darling, as long as you love me too.
I promised we'll be tied together.
This is my pledge to you.
I promised, I promised,
I promised.

THE LAST KISS

She was the one, who took my virginity,
But we couldn't continue anymore.
We gave up on each other for eternity.
The anger that existed must end forevermore.
I gave her my last kiss,
But she never believed I was sore.
But in reality I was pissed.
I said to her, "I couldn't handle it anymore."

I said to her, "I don't like this.
I hate to be at war.
I would like to give you a last kiss."
But she still not believed I was sore.

The first time we met.
She walked toward me and held my hand.
Then gave me a closed-mouth kiss,
Ah! That first kiss was wet.
I didn't feel the earth I stand.
We were both carried away with the kiss.
That kiss to me had been planned.
Her presence in my life was bliss.

That last kiss too I would never forget
The last kiss lasted for a short duration.
It was very dry. It wasn't wet.
The kiss has no sensation.
I was sweat.
Sweat from love's frustration.
For that last kiss was a kiss of threat.

I gave her that last touch of the lips.
I could not continue to be in chain.
Then I went and wrote it on my script.
Forever I didn't want to love a woman again.
My heart was ripped.
I gave her a goodbye kiss, and it was forever.
For loving a woman I was whipped.
Then I said, "A woman again—never, no never!"

YOUR LOVE

Is to me like magic, darling.
I hope I had met you long ago.
Each time I think of you,
I dance in ballet dance,
I dance ballroom like a macho.
I dance belly dance.

Dance with me, darling,
Make me feel like a macho.
Dance with me darling,
You're my only hope.
Dance with me, darling,
Make me feel like a man,
Dance with me, darling,
You're my only woman.

Each time I think of you,
I remember the first day we met.
And I knew that you were born for me.
Even in my dream when I think you,
I dance exotic and hula dance.
And hip as I sweat.

Don't you notice?
In every word that I speak,
I must say, I love you in Greek.
And I began to dance Isuzu,
And tap dance.
As we bind in love.

Oh darling, each time I think
Of your magic love,
I dance country and western
I dance break dance
I dance like a dove.
Your love to me is like magic.

IF I FIND MY WOMAN

I would treat her as a queen.
We will always dress in jeans.
She knows how to love a man.
I've seen men on the lookout for such a woman.
She makes a man run like an ant after her.
She uses her mind to make her man
Go on his knees and run after her.

Quand je la trouve
Je veux vivre pour elle,
Quand elle me trouve
Elle veut vivre pour moi,
My woman and me,
Nous voulons vivre l'un pour l'autre.

If I find her, I will be in love for the rest of my life.
And forever I will make her my wife.
She will know how to use her fingers to make a good meal.
I have been on the lookout for such a real
And rare woman, a fine lady with such an appeal.
Such a matron to me is a big deal.

Quand je la trouve
Je veux vivre pour elle,
Quand elle me trouve
Elle veut vivre pour moi,
My woman and me,
Nous voulons vivre l'un pour l'autre.

WHEN YOU LOVE SOMEONE

Not the fine regards that she holds.
Nor the princely look that he unfolds.
But you listen to her splendid words of love.
And treat her well thereof.

Not when she wears her exquisite dress.
Not when he wears he jaunty livery and has a big chess.
But you understand when he nods his head.
And appreciate everything he said.

You love him even when he can't give money.
You love her if even when she is not too funny.
And you feel dispirited when his not at his best time.
You always love her even if she can't afford a dime.

You love her not for the nice food she can cook.
You love him not for his nice look.
Each moment you spend together is God given.
When you love someone, you learn to be forgiven.

MY HEART FOR CHRISTMAS

The best thing I can give you is my heart for Christmas.
I love you from the bottom of my heart.
Let go to Mass, we'll share the love of Christ.
I will pray to God for you in my part.
My friend, let go to Mass to pray for each other on Christmas.

As a friend with all my heart I cherish you.
I really do.
I want to share the love of Christ with you, when you go to Mass.
I wish you a merry Christmas.
I promise you, my love; I will go to Mass,
And I will pray for you too.

I'm certain God put in your heart to love me too.
I promise I will go to Mass.
Oh yeah, my darling, I will do.
I will go to Mass,
I will pray for you too.
The best I can give you is my heart for Christmas.

I LOVE YOU SO MUCH

I love you so much, when I think of you,
I fall to sleep by you touching and caressing me.
Your magic touch is like voodoo.
When I look at your eyes, love is the only thing I see.
Your presence is worth more than gold and your love is long overdue.
I love when you are touching me from head to toes to put me in deep sleep at your chest.
My tongue is insufficient to express my love for you.
When I am sleeping on your chest I feel like a little bird in the nest.

Your touch is like voodoo and when I am with you I fill with mirth.
I love touching your hair and sucking your breast.
It is for you that God sent me to earth.
When I am sleeping on your chest, I feel like a little bird at rest.
My tongue is insufficient to express my love for you.
Your magic touch is like voodoo to me.
Your magic touch makes me inflame with love too.
And when I look at your eyes, love is the only thing I see.

When I am by you, I am teeming with love.
My lover, touch me, put me on your chest.
Your touch makes me become a dove.
Who can ever love like you? You will always be the best.
It is when I met you I began to burgeon.
When you speak I become a bird on my nest, repose.
Your touch is the only medicine that makes me feel calm; you are my surgeon.
Put me on your chest, I will fall asleep, then touch me from head to toes.

YOU ARE MY IDLE

Your jocund nature makes me fall in love with you.
You are an idle for me too.
Every time you smile, I feel like falling down at your feet.
You are great and sweet.

The alacrity that you bring in my life makes me feel complete.
Your jocund nature makes me fall at your feet.
Oh! You have such a fervent belief in love.
Darling, you are my dove.

Your presence to me is stronger than incense.
When you talk, your words make sense.
You are my joy.
I'd love to play with you like a toy.

You are my hope and make my life complete.
Your jocund nature makes me fall at your feet.
Darling, you are my dove and my scope.
You are my idol and my only hope.

NOW I KNOW YOU LOVE ME

Your friends say to you I am foolish and that you should leave me.

Oh! My darling, I love you more when you answer, "Let him be."

Then you come to me and say you will never leave me.

Then I say to you, darling, now and forever I love thee.

My gracious sweetheart, now I know you love me.

Your sagacious personality makes me appreciate thee.

Your comrade said to you, "Leave the perfidious," but you stay with me.

Oh! Gracious sweetheart, now you know, I believe in thee.

They ask, "Why do you stay with a man so poor?

He is careless and immature."

You never listen to them and before their eyes you said to me, "I love thee."

Ah! My gracious sweetheart, now I know, you love me.

They say, "If you get sick, this man cannot buy you insure.

And he is insecure."

Above all, I lost my job, but you stick with me.

My gracious love, now I must love thee.

In sickness and till death, I will always love thee.

In moment of distress and danger, you promised to be with me.

If you fall, unable to get up, I will carry thee.

Trust me, my gracious love, I will always love thee.

COME HERE, MY LOVE!

Or do you want me to come to you, my dear?
I will drive the Jaguar
I will come to stand by your fence.
I will play the guitar,
And together we will dance,
Yeah! We will dance without fear.

Darling, will you not punish me?
You are my only sweetheart.
You are the only one that can set me free
From the prison of love in your part,
Don't give me a broken heart.

Darling, I'm at your door praying.
Open your heart and give me a chance to be your lover.
I'm singing.
Listen to your lover playing the guitar, when I come over.
You are my redeemer.
Save me, my dear, from dying for scrap of love.

Oh darling, you change my life
By not depriving me of your love, my dear.
For your love I will always feel starved.
Let me play for you my guitar.
Yeah, my precious! This beautiful day will engrave
In my heart till I die, my dear.

Oh darling, let me come by your fence.
I will come out of my Jaguar.
I will stand by your fence.
I will play my guitar,
You and I will dance,
Dance and dance for the world to see, my dear,
We are in love.

YOUR TOUCH IS LIKE MAGIC

I'm sleepless without you, baby, by my side,
When you are touching me, I feel bliss.
That's when I say, "O la, la! O, la, la, la!"
I love when you give me a sweet kiss,
As you say, "O la, la! O la, la!"
Then I say, "Touch this!"
And you say, "I love you de tout mon coeur.
De tout mon coeur."

Darling, you're a littérateur.
You came and sat by my side.
Darling, you are an amateur.
As you sat beside
Me and said, "Ta la, la! Ta la, la!"
You told me, "You're an amateur"
"You're an amateur."
Then I said: "O la, la! O la, la!
O la, la! O la, la!"

You came to me and said,
"You drive me crazy!"
"You drive me crazy!"
Then I said:
"I'm not a chauffeur."
"I'm not a chauffeur."
"How do I drive you crazy?"

You dance for me,
As you sing: Pa la, la! Pa la, la!
You make me feel good!
You put me in the good mood.
As I say, "Ta la, la! Ta la, la!"
Your touch is like magic.
How can I stop loving you?
De tout mon coeur,
De tout mon coeur.

A BITTER UNION

Blame yourself,
Folks said no,
Sisters and brothers said no,
Friends and everybody said no,
But you insisted to kill yourself.
You must accept the blow.
Nay is the gift of the intelligent.

Tears won't dry from your eyes.
You will cry, cry, and cry again.
You will cry, you weren't wise.
Everything you own will go to the drain,
You were not wise.
You should suffer with your pain.

Since you're a man,
Tears won't dry from your eyes.
Your trouble just began.
Blame it on yourself, and accept your prize.
You should have been wise.
You will cry until you get tired, man!
Your help won't even come from the skies.

GET WET

I love to get wet.
I ran to the rain with my suit on.
Oh! I feel no fret.
Getting wet to me is fun.
I get soaked and wet.
As the rain falls like music to my ear
I dance and play in it with no fret.
It makes me cheery.
Each time you touch me,
I get wet.
It's like I jump into the river or the sea.
Oh! I feel no fret.
I jumped into the pool of love
Oh! Ah! I love to get wet.
I feel like a wet dove.
I get wet like in the rain without fret.
Especially when it is not covered with that glove.

BEFORE I MET YOU

I had a dream: you came on my way.
I had no hope when you came to say
You love me and told me that you gave me your heart.
I told you I give you my soul in my part.

You alone my heart desires.
You are alone that I truly love.
Your love enters my heart like fire.
You alone can make me feel love.

I had a dream that you were glad I came on your way.
You had lost hope when I came to say
I love you and I would give you my heart.
You told me that you would give your soul in your part.

LIKE A BABY

You held me like a baby.
You caressed and dodo me like a baby.
I feel your love in my mind and soul.
Your touch makes me feel love in my soul.

Uh baby! Why touch me there?
Uh baby! Why kissed me there!
Uh baby! Your love moves each of my hair.
Like a baby is hungry for milk, so I am for your love.

Oh! darling, hold me again like a baby if you would.
Make me feel good.
Uh darling! You make me feel sweet.
Your love enters my soul and warms me like a heat.

THE SOUND OF LOVE

Uh! I hear something coming; it is the sound of love.
Uh! I see something coming; it is look likes love.
Uh! Something in the air, it smells likes love.
Uh! Something is in my mouth; it tastes likes love.
Uh! Something I touch; it is as hot as love.

Love is like the sea,
When it exists, it is deep and wide.
Love is like the heaven above that I can see
When it exists, it is high and can be seen worldwide.
Love is like the moon above the earth and the sea,
When it exists, it is bright outside.

Love is color-blind.
Love is not selfish and it's kind.
Love is never shy.
Love believes in goodness and it's not dry.
Love is above all things.
Love is not prejudice and it's always kind.

I CAN EVER LIVE WITHOUT YOU

If combined all the stars in the sky,
Your presence is brighter to me than the sun in the sky.
Like a deer seeking for water in the desert without you I will die.
So I am dying for your love, come to me don't be shy.

I dream of you 365 days a year.
Just as the lilies are praying for the rain, so I want you to make me cheer.
My heart desires to hear you say you love me, your voice always sounds new.
You are the treasure that I am searching, I hope to find you.

Sometimes I am awake in the middle of the night,
It's like you are in the bed caressing me at night.
My soul always wondering about you,
Every time I hear your voice, it sounds new.

I always cry when I don't see you in the morning, I swear.
It's like the sun never rises and I feel no air.
You are as beautiful as a teddy bear
You are more precious than diamond and gold, I swear.

Oh, how I love you touching me.
Oh, how precious you are to me.
You alone are my heart desire and love.
You alone are my dove.

I love you every second and I dream of you at night.
I'd love you caressing me every minute at night.
I love you every hour and you are always in my prayer.
I dream you every day, I swear.
Because you alone I love, your love to me is like the air.

NUDE BY THE POND

I stood by the pond; it was calm and sweet.
But I realized the little pond next to it had been gone.
In my heart I asked, how could that be?
I realized that the larger pond swallowed the small one, I withdrew.
Somewhat from that spite, I was afraid not to sink in that zone.
Then suddenly, I saw a frog stand on top of a white stone.

Then I saw a huge snake sat, calm inside the large pond.
All of a sudden, the frog tried to move from the white stone.
I heard my brother call, but I stayed calm, did not respond.
Suddenly, the snake jumped on the frog and the frog was gone.
I was amazed and continued to watch beyond.
The pond, the water was calm and sweet.

I could not believe all the changes I saw as I continued to gaze.
Then I saw a man came and took off his clothes and stayed nude.
Nude as when he came from his mother's womb, how amazing.
He looked like a fifteenth-century statue of Goltzius but in a good mood.
I watched his muscles; it was like seeing King Alexander standing nude.
His noble face looked like watching President Clinton and Monica Lewinsky nude.

Then, I saw a woman, she looked like my mother standing by a palm tree.
Ah . . . that's must be my father, I can't let them see me or it's rude.
The woman called to the man, "Do you see me?"
The man signaled to the woman to come, as she was nude
Then the man came on top of the woman and he was nude
Then the man began to dance, the woman played a guitar, he was nude
As he was twisting his posterior like a mosquito playing a tambourine, nude.

BEAUTIFUL

You are beautiful and your eyes shine with love.
When you sit next to me, your presence is like dew,
It makes me fresh like a plant by the river, you're a dove.
I produce good fruits because of you, thank you.

You are like the lilies grow on the yard of the president.
They are beautiful and sweet.
So, come to sit with me in the mist of the lilies where I'm a resident.
You are my fragrance, come to me, take a seat.

When I hear your voice, I feel the sun rises in my heart.
Like the sun, you make me feel warm.
I feel safe by your side; I feel you are closer to my heart.
Like eaglet feel safe under the wing of a mother eagle, so I am under your arm.

Your love makes me feel glad.
You are as beautiful as the queen of Sheba, you never look sad
Your dresses are made in France
And your perfumes give me a chance.

When you touch me, your hands are as sweet as honeycomb.
Touch me more so I can move closer and closer to you.
Talk to me, your voice sounds like the queens of Rome
Rubbed by King Cesar and your touch makes me feel good too.

I am yours and you are mine. Come to me like my little chick
Eat corn in my soft hand, your touch makes my blood shiver, you're my chick.
At night, come to my door and I will find you a place to sleep,
When spring starts, come to sit with me in the breeze.

WHERE IS THE LOVE

You told me that you love me,
But you don't feel like you owed me any respect.
You told me that you cared for me,
But you showed to me disrespect.

I gave you love,
I received hate.
I put you above
Everything and at any rate.

I gave you my time,
But you gave me deception
I see it as a crime,
And I hope you change your perception.

I am looking for mutual consent,
You want to take charge and you never were content.
I want us to be happy, but you make me lament.
You want yourself to be happy and put others in torment.

I forgive you and I really do,
But you hold me countable with good intent.
Doesn't God give you a sense to care for others too?
You could take a little of my content
Or I will escape from your grips too.

JUNE 1998

June 1998 was the month and the year my woman threw me out.
June 1998 was the month I learned that you loved me with no doubt.
June 1998 you took me under your bosom and put me to sleep in the mist of your legs.
In the morning, you prepared me the best scrambled eggs.
I swear before God of trinity in June 1998, I tasted real love.
Yeah! In June 1998 I tasted true love from my only beloved.

We never knew that we love each other until June 1998 it was proved.
You never told me that you love me, but you action on June 1998 testified.
June 1998 you taught me real love that in my heart will never be removed.
June 1998 I learned that real love can't be hidden and our love is justified.
I swear before Jehovah God, real love is between two best friends.
And nothing can stop me from loving you till the end.

After June 1998 whenever you pass near me I could smell love.
Whenever you give me a hug, I could feel love.
Whenever I looked at you I see love.
Whenever I drank in the cup you had drunk, I tasted love.
I swear before God, you are the only one I ever love.

In my mind, you are the only true being that God ever created.
You are the only one my heart meditating. My love for you is unlimited.
When I don't see you, I don't eat day and night I think of your sweet breath.
Since '98, you have been my only focus. I think of you as soft spirited.
I swear before God almighty, I love you to death.

Since June 1998, I have been in love with you.
You have become an idle for me.
I have tried to hide it from you,
But love can never be hidden—you caught me.
Yeah, now you know, till death I love you.

AUGUST 1998

August 1998, I remember it like today.
I told you after a month together that I was leaving with tears in my eyes.
You asked me to please stay.
I looked at your awesome face and began to cry.
Then I saw tears dropping down like rain from your eyes.
I swear to God, your charm and kindness came to me as a surprise.

While I was contemplating your beauty and wisdom, you made me beef stew.
I drank the best juice that you made and ate with you.
Then you hugged me goodbye and I felt your warm and sweet breath.
I pressed you, I touched you, and then you knew that my heart stayed with you.
You gave me a pen and asked me to write my address and date of birth.
I swear before God almighty! Since that July 1998 my heart belonged to you.

After that you called me and told me that you love me till the end.
I took a piece of paper, I wrote your name in large print with a pen.
Again, I heard your sweet voice leaving me a message in my voicemail.
Oh! It was so sweet just like the voice of Angel Gabriel, and it has become my tale.
Oh how sweet, listening to your voice again and gain.
You are a beauty, a being with a good brain.

After that I received a note from you.
The note says, "I love you to death too."
Oh! How sweet! You put a little perfume in the note.
I read the sweet and heartfelt note that you wrote.
I smelled the sweet perfume and thought of you.
I wrote you a note back with a little perfume, the note says, "I love you too."

Every night I dream of you and me sitting by the sea.
As you are already aware, in my dream you are the only one I see.
You are like a lover, like a sweetheart, you are meek.
The rest of my life is to love you day after day and week after week.
You know that I love you, but I don't always tell you that face-to-face.
But with paper and ink, I write, "You are an amazing grace."

NOVEMBER 2003

In my home I was confined.
Most of the time I stayed inside.
I looked at the window, then I saw you at my door.
Oh my! What a wonderful suit you wore!
I thought you were an angel descending from the heaven above.
I said, "O, my God! Here is the one I love!"

I ran to meet you outside, listened to your sweet voice that always makes me cry.
I opened the door, then you came inside.
My heart was beating when I saw your graceful face.
Your presence at my residence was an amazing grace.
I believe that God created you just for me and it came to my mind on that day.
And it is my reason to love you and with you I will always want to stay.

DON'T BE IMMATURE

I thought you were smart or you would love me.
You would want to caress a man like me.
You would want to be with a man like me.
I would make love with you every night.
I would caress you every morning and hold you in my arms.
I would touch you, make you feel sweet and hold you tight.
I would make you feel like you are in heaven and you would be glad.
I am kind. I am sweet. I am a strong man.
I am unbeatable when it comes to love. I am charming. I won't make you mad.
I am not arrogant. Chose me and learn how to be in love with a real man.

AT YOUR FEET I FOUND MY SPOT

It is at your feet I found my spot.
When those long, brown hairy legs set on my lap,
Your toes are as sweet as an apricot.
I am always missing them when they are not on my lap.
Your feet are my spot.
I love to touch, kiss, and hold them as my lad.
And suck them as a sweet apricot.
Your legs are forever beautiful and they make me glad.
Your legs are always turning me on.
I love to put lotion on them.
I can spend my life in those legs like an ice-cream cone.
I can never stop looking and caressing them.
Just your feet, it is all I want as my spot.
Your entire body turns me on, but your legs, I love them.
It is in your brown, sexy, and hairy legs I found my spot.

I LOST AFTER YOU

Every morning I am watching you
As you are leaving for work.
I lost after you and I spend all day searching for your name on Yahoo.
You are always in my mind.
You are the most beautiful among mankind.
Your shining eyes make me feel like a bachelor.
I hope you could be mine,
I hope I could be yours.
When I go to bed, I keep looking for you,
But I can't find you. I want to be yours.
God forbid, if I can't find you,
I am going crazy for you,
But if I find you I will take you to my bed.
I will show you that nobody ever loved you like I do.

LIKE A COCONUT TREE

The one that I love is like my coconut tree that my grandfather planted for me.
There are always plenty of coconuts in it.
Oh! I will drink water from my coconuts with my sweetheart tonight.
So my lover is as rich as a honeybee.
My lover always makes me feel sweet in the middle of the night.

Every morning I wake up to admire my beautiful coconut
Tree that reminds me of the one that I cherish.
Oh! She is stunning in her wet suit.
Oh my love! I am weak, of too much passion. I cherish
You, put your hand around me, make me sweet like the coconut.

You are the one who makes me feel sweet at night.
Caress me, my dear, and touch me everywhere
I swear! You deserve my joy; I will give you all tonight.
Your lips are as beautiful as a golden chandelier.
Restore my strengths with your soft kiss tonight.

Oh my sweetheart, how can I stop loving you?
Every night I only dream about you.
You are the only one that pleases me.
You are the only one that satisfies me.
You are handsome. I love your shining eyes too.

YOU REMIND ME OF MOUNT MOREAU

Oh darling, you remind me of Mount Moreau where I used to stand to watch the sea.
Moro is where I first tasted breadfruit.
It is where my father met his first girlfriend Rosalie,
She is a beautiful woman who came from Family Jesuit.

You have the scent of the mint in my mother's garden.
Uh darling! Your love is better than all the wealth on earth.
Oh! I fell in love with you when I was thirteen and you were fourteen.
I pray to God to bless the day of your birth.

Darling! Where do you go after work tonight?
I will go look for you among the actresses on Broadway.
I hope you could always be on my sight.
And I am delighted that God has sent you on my way.

I will listen to your voice singing like an angel from heaven.
Believe, my dear, nobody else on earth is as beautiful as you are.
I swear to God, when I saw you I thought you were an angel from heaven.
Someone such as beautiful and passionate like you is rare.

Promise me, my dear, and swear to God that I will always be your lover.
Promise me that you will always be close to me.
And I will go riding hoses with you as a great cavalier.
I promised you, my dear, my love for you is guarantee.
You will be my best friend and lover forever.

OH! YOU ARE LOOKING FOR ME

It was to my surprise, when I opened the door
I saw you standing behind it, I knew you were looking for me.
I said, "Here is the one that I adore!
Here is my lover, the one that I could not wait to see."

My hair vibrated and my blood moved inside me.
Then you came, drank a cup of chocolate with me.
Then you gave me a kiss that was sweeter than the chocolate.
You told me, "Darling, I prefer a cup of sweet tea."
And I said, "Darling, drink me, I am your cup of tea.

Oh it was so sweet listen to the voice that I love the most.
It was marvelous caressing and hugging the one I cherish.
I remember you wore a beautiful leather coat.
Oh! On that day I spent my time to prepare you my best dish.

I put my hand around you and pressed your breast.
You are the most passionate.
I never found one like you in the past.
Darling, you are my chocolate.
You are filled with caress, passion, love and you have a sweet breast.

LOVE IS A DIFFICULT THING

Loving someone is one thing,
But finding the right person to love is another.
A lover can become a sting.
If one finds your weaknesses, instead of giving you love, he hates you rather.
Sometimes, the one you love is looking for a chance to sting
You like a bee.

Love can be a difficult thing.
You cannot always tell one that you are in love with him.
You lost sleep after him as if you spend the night watching a king.
You never have time to rest by watching him even in the gym.
But the one that you love never thinks of you even as a thing.

DON'T LOOK DOWN ON A WOMAN

Woman
Ah! Darling, why have you done that? Don't you think it's a mistake
To look down on a woman like me as if I am a snake?
I don't have the best lotions to put on me, but I know what I can make.
Inside me, I am an attractive woman and know how to make a cake.
My lips are sweet even though I don't have the most attractive dress,
My kisses are smooth and if you find me, you will be blessed.

Man
Ah! Darling, you don't look like your kisses can be as sweet as honey from a honeybee.
You do not look as if you can make a man feel sweet to me.
I had to look down on thee?
I am looking for a woman that looks beautiful outside.
I am looking for a woman that I can show to my friends as my bride.
I am looking for a woman that can be seen as attractive worldwide.

Woman
Never look down on a woman that appears hideous to you.
She might become the most attractive and the sweetest bride.
Beautiful woman may look attractive outside,
But inside she might be a sorrow too.
Ask me and I will tell you how men fall when they are too proud.
A beautiful woman can be as bitter as vinegar too.

Man
Tell me, tell me, darling, how a man might fall.
Good women are always appearing pretty?
Good women are beautiful and tall?
Good women are from noble families in the city?
Good women are have the sweetest lips of all?

Woman

A man might fall as he begins to compliment a woman for her charm.
He notices her outside appearance and begins to kiss her in the arm.
But every woman is a mystery, unless a man is intelligent, he might get harm.
Only God knows who is delightful and pretty.
Never look down on a woman that appears hideous to you.
Good women are not always from the noble families in the city.
A beautiful woman can be as bitter as vinegar too.

Man

A beautiful woman won't make my mouth bitter and it is a woman like you.
A beautiful woman won't cause pain to a man and she makes one feel sure.
A beautiful woman is not a woman that looks attractive worldwide.
A beautiful woman is a woman like you that keeps her dignity and I make you my bride.

EVER SINCE I MET YOU

I have been in love with you since day one.
Every word you speak has a sweet taste in my mouth.
Your words put joy in my heart and you always sound fun.
Your voice sounds as beautiful as one from the south.

You are the only one I need.
When I am needing something to drink,
It seems that you are the one I need.
When I am hungry only about you I think.
I love you and you are the only one I need.

You are my hope.
I love you, for you fear the Lord.
You are my hope.
I love you for my heart and yours are in accord.
I love you, because you love me and you are my only hope.

NEVER THINK YOUR PARTNER IS STUPID

Darling, I am not stupid, trust me, I love you.
Darling, take my word and wear it in your neck.
My name is Wisdom put me in your mouth and chew.
I can be as sweet as honey and you can put me in the bank as a good check.

Darling, listen to what I have to tell you:
Never try to take advantage of your lover.
Never take advantage of your partner who cares for you.
You might think he is stupid, but an undercover.
When you're sincere to your partner, benediction will come down to you like dew.

IT IS YOUR LOVE

It is not magic that you carry out,
But when at your presence, I feel like the sun is rising in my heart.
It is not magic that you did to make me feel that you are the only one that helped
me out,
But when I am at your presence, I feel the rain is falling in my heart.
It is your love that flourishes in my heart like a garden without a doubt.

Every time I see you,
I feel a breeze that comes to give me fresh air.
You warm me up too.
I was sad when you came to my life to give me joy, and someone like you is rare.
Oh, what a sun you bring to my soul every time you touch me there.
It gives me joy and makes everyone look at me.
It is your love that brings me delight and it is for your love only I care.
It is your love that set me free.

MARRIAGE

There are no words to define the charm that brings a couple into marriage.
When two people are in love, it is like a chandelier that never turns off.
They are bound to each other and with each other they will never disparage.
And you are a perfect match that God created and He will carry your vow through.

Marriage is the oath made between two people before man and God.
God united them to care and to love each other.
You're swearing before God to give all yourself with no façade
To your partner, to protect and love one another.

Mankind, God, and his angels get together
Today to recognize you in marriage.
Now you can play even in bed in good and bad weather.
God and his angels will never leave you alone to get disparage.

Now together you can do all.
The presence of God almighty is with you today and forever.
The spirit of God will remind you to never let each other fall
Just surrender to our God of peace that reigns forever.

BY YOUR LOVE YOU CAPTURED MY SOUL

You are a golden lampstand
You're always lit in my heart and you always look bright.
I always see you standing in my heart as a golden lampstand.
Your love is the oil that gives me joy at night.

I feel sweet when you touch me with your gentle hands.
You kiss me with you soft lips.
You allow me to touch your secret place without demands.
You allow me kiss and touch even your hips.

My love for you is deep.
Your touch transports my soul into deep sleep.
The heaven that you created in my mind.
By your love you capture my soul and put me to sleep.
You are a treasure that I find.

I LIVE FOR YOU ALONE

When I sit, you are sitting on a bench in my mind.
When I walk, you are walking with me.
I never spend a moment without you, the angel I find.
Wherever I go, your face goes with me.
I never love anyone else like you and you are so kind.
It is for you that I lost all my sleep, because you are the only one I see.
I live for you and for you alone among mankind.
I hope you can tell me that you love me.

YOU ARE FINALLY MINE

I have been praying to God so that you could be mine.
Today before God and mankind you swear to be mine.
I swear to be yours.
In marriage we are united in love.

You are a dream come true.
Now you not only live in my heart and mind.
You can touch me as I caress you.
It is God above that united us in love.

You ask me to be your husband.
I ask you to be my wife.
You are forever my sweet love.
I am forever your sweet charm.

WHEN YOU PROPOSED TO ME

I said yes to you that I love you.
Since you came to my life, my life has been complete.
Nobody else would ever make me so blessed when my life was blue.
I am happy in your arm and you're always making me feel sweet.

You are an angel in my life. I love to be at your feet.
I need you to know, without your charm, my life is incomplete.
You give me love that nobody else could ever give me. Oh! How sweet!
Oh! How can I love you more! You make my life complete.

I WILL NEVER LOVE AGAIN

When you left me, I knew what I was missing,
But I didn't care to lose someone who loved to cheat.
I didn't care about missing your kissing.
I didn't care anymore; you had been a complete deceit.

You gave me a broken heart again and again.
After what you had done to me, I would not trust someone again.
I would never say to someone, "I love you" again.
I swear to God you caused me lot of pain.
And why should I let someone break my heart again?

I AM SORRY TO ASK FOR ALL THIS ATTENTION

It is because I love you and I want to be close to you.
When you came to my life, you became a lamp on my feet.
You were as shining as the sun, and know how to make love too.

My days became bright.
My nights were no longer gruesome.
You were like an angel watching over my soul at night.

I love you and your love gives me a new dimension.
Your touch is what makes me want to live for you.
I am sorry to ask for all this attention.
But it is because I love you.

BY YOUR SIDE

By your side,
I'm cheering and blissful.
By your side,
I feel grateful.
And I love for you to be my bride.

By your side
I will never feel hungry if you become my bride.
By your side
It's where I love to be.
I feel bless that you love me.

By your side I find comfort.
I wish I could always be by your side forever.
With your love I never have discomfort.
You are a great lover.

GOOD MORNING, BEAUTIFUL LADY

Good morning, beautiful lady, you look charming today.
I have seen you passing by every morning; your shining eyes awake me.
My mother and my father told me they have seen you every day.
They asked for me to ask you to be my lover even if I have to go on my knee.

Oh dear, last night I had a dream, I saw you.
I asked you if you loved me and you told me that you do.
You are as beautiful as a wild flower and I am the dew.
I know you father and mother, I'd love to marry you.

Oh dear! I've seen you with a bucket in your hand every day.
What have you done with all the water that you drew?
I love to go with you by the bay.
Know that you mother and father won't stop me from loving you.

Sir, I draw water for my mother, she is poor
She is busy working hard to support us
I try to understand her; I don't want to be immature,
I can understand that she is working hard for success.

Miss, you are doing well helping your mother.
Let me help you carry the bucket, I will feel blessed.
You are beautiful too; I hope I was your brother.
I would get a chance to see you all time to caress.

I am too young, sir, to talk about caress.
I have no father; my mother works hard to pay for food.
My mother is working hard for my success.
I have no time for love and please do not think that I am rude.

Let me come with you, my dear.
I love to kiss you and caress you.
I will give you my love to make you cheer.
I know that you have kept your dignity too.
I know that you are a bottle of wine, my dear.

Oh my dear, I will drink your wine.
You sweet wine is the only thing I desire.
I am taking you to the home that I have built and you will be mine.
I promise you, darling, that I love you, I am not a liar.
I promise you, darling, with me you will always be fine.

NO WONDER WHY I LOVE YOU

No wonder why I love you.
You have been there for me in all respects,
And I know that you are honest for sure.
There is an atmosphere of trust between us in every aspect.

I love you for your high work ethic.
I love you for your dedication.
You are always willing to listen and you are chic.
You always listen to my ideas by your education.
You accept my criticism and sometimes they are not nice.

You teach me how to grow.
You never get angry even when I hurt you.
You help me when I was in sorrow.
How can I ever leave one that loves me for sure?

MY SOUL DREAMS OF YOU

I can't think of anyone else but you.
You have been the center of my life.
You are the only being on earth in my view.
I think of you day and night, you are the center of my life.

Every time I try to plunge into sleep,
I hear your sweet voice calling me,
"Joe, Joe, my sweetheart," and in my dream I weep.
I love you; you were created for me.

I always sleep with you even when you are afar.
My mind only thinks of your beautiful body.
My soul thinks of your sweet breast.
I love to hear your voice; you are not like anybody.

You have been sweeter to me than honey.
Without your touch I can't fall asleep at night.
Your sweet caress worth more than money.
My soul will never stop dreaming of you at night.

When you fondle me, I always fall asleep.
You alone my heart desires, besides the God above.
Your perfect lips always put me to sleep.
You alone I want to live with and you alone I love.

MY ONLY DESIRE

My desire is to love you anyhow.
To love you forever is my only vow.
I swear to God if you leave me I will have a breakdown.
You are always in my mind from morning to sundown.

My desire began when you touch me from behind.
Whenever you touch me, you take control of my mind.
God knows that my heart and mind only think of you.
I hope you think of me too.

I love you because I know your heart is with me.
Your actions prove your love for me.
I swear to God if you leave me I will die.
Forever, you and I will be closer and with you I will abide.

I love the way you talk about us, you always say, "We."
And you never hide anything from me.
I swear to God almighty, I can't live without you.
And I know you can't live without me too.

Your touch makes me feel sweet; it's like I have been carried with the wind.
When I am irate, my dear, just a touch will make me surrender all.
Your touch filled my soul with joy, especially when you touched me from behind.
Oh darling! Your touch takes control of my heart, mind, and soul.

YOUR SWEET VOICE

Your sweet voice gives me strength day after day.
Your voice always sounds sweet and kind.
It's God alone that could put someone like you on my way.
Your voice flourishes the garden of my heart, and it clears my mind.

Your voice is like the rain, it burgeons me up.
When you speak in my ear, your voice is an art.
Your voice is like the sun, it warms me up.
To me you are a great hero and smart.

This morning I saw you,
My soul danced inside me as I was listening to your literature.
My spirit awaked at your presence too.
You make my life complete and I keep you in my d'amour.

At your presence I always love to be.
You give me hope to live another day.
You are my daily joy, my heart long for thee.
You make my life complete as I always say.

HOW BEAUTIFUL

It's awesome when young people are in love and believe in holiness.
They have no experience in love but believe in God faithfulness.
They will celebrate love with a whole community.
These young people can be looked at as good examples in society.

In my youth I relied on God's faithfulness.
I never had to be reminded to stay away from sin.
I wanted the world to celebrate my youthfulness.
I knew from my parents that sin brings chagrin.

When I was young I listened to my folks.
Who dared to ask me to commit fornication?
I was glad when the entire neighborhood came and congratulated me.
I learned that abstinence is no joke.

If young people want to make it, they need to pray.
Abstinence requires an entire community to teach the young about real love.
Yeah it is beautiful when two young people wait after the wedding to make love.
"You do the right thing, boys and girls," I would say.

ANOTHER MAN IN THE MIRROR

Oh! It is very sad when you look at your old self in a mirror.
I thought it was part of my genetic code to make a woman sing for me.
To any man I thought I would never have been inferior.
I got in the mist of her legs and afterward she applauded me.

Now I am looking at me in a mirror.
In my old pictures I see my handsome face.
Yeah! To these young men today, I am an inferior.
God created love, I invented true love, but I can no longer continue the race.

When I look at my beautiful black hair,
I am still handsome, but I can't take a blank check.
But now my beautiful hair is theirs.
Now I am unable to do my job, I am a jerk.

I look at myself in a mirror; my white teeth came to mind.
I look at myself in a mirror; it is my endurance that engrave.
I am now near death, and my endurance I don't have.
It is something every woman would hope to find.

A BEAUTIFUL STATUETTE

The soccer game just started; then appeared a statuette.
I could not resist from getting myself wet.
So other creatures like me also got wet.
It is only God that can make such a statuette.

I heard a male creature who sat behind me said, "She from Singapore."
I said, "Wow! This football game I shall never regret."
Before I presented myself to the statuette I went to look at me in a mirror.
By the time I got back another creature just like me sat next to the statuette.

I went to thank God for such a creature that only he could create.
She was the most beautiful being on earth.
I got wet each time I looked at the creature that only God could create.
I had never in my life seen such a creature since my birth.

Another time I watched the statuette sleep.
I could not tell her that I loved her yet.
But every time I saw her I got wet.
Oh! She was the most beautiful creature that I ever met.

LIFE IS WORTH LIVING

When I am sitting alone with a beauty like you playing with my toy.
You are so sweet; I can't live without your love.
Even the angels come to watch us when we are making love.
Yeah! Your presence to me is a joy.

Oh how great! Sitting with the one I love eating honey with a silver spoon.
Nothing is as beautiful as you, not even the moon.
You are sweet and you are my pilot.
You are beautiful and you are hot.

Life is beautiful when you and I watch the wind carry the leaves.
Then we are listening to birds singing thereof.
Oh my dear, give me more of your love.
Oh my dear! I love when you put your hand through my sleeves.

Oh darling, life is worth living when I have someone like you to love.
You are a gift given to me by God above.
When you and I together in love life is fun.
You are a perfect prize that I won.

YOU AND I IN LOVE FOREVER

Because you love me you put me above everything.
Because I love you I put you above everything.
You walk with me hand in hand while we're articulating about love.
Oh my sweetheart, let make love.

You and I are in love forever.
I will never, never leave you.
You are mine forever.
Because I love you and you love me too.

I remember when you called me last night.
You went to New York just for the night,
But I could not sleep because I was thinking of you.
I sat on my bed all night remembering you.

I am praying to God to bring you back to me.
I am praying to God to give you joy.
You are the only one I want to see,
Hurry, come back so you can play with my toy.

I feel you present all the time.
I love to play with your toy.
I love you for a lifetime.
Because you are the one who gives me joy.

Darling, each time I think of you, I feel a complete joy.
Your presence fills my heart with gladness.
At night you put me to sleep in the mist of your breast like a boy.
You take away all my sadness.

I LOVE YOU FOR A LIFETIME

Darling, I love you for a lifetime.
Even when you are far I feel your presence all the time.
Because of you I am always living with hope.
You are my only scope.

You are full of joy and you are beautiful.
I love you, my wonderful.
Your presence fills my heart with gladness.
I love you, my dear, for your faithfulness.

You put me to sleep in the mist of your breast at night.
Oh! I am glad I will pass my time with you tonight.
I hope you will be closer to me at all times,
Then I would not have to sleep without you sometimes.

I MUST THANK GOD

I must thank God.
He gave you to me and me to you.
Your presence in my life is a great reward.
I must appreciate and love you too.

I must thank God.
Who am I to sit on a table with you?
Who am I to have someone like you to speak in one accord?
Sometimes you lay me too.

I must thank God.

RUB ME AS YOU DID LAST NIGHT

It is raining tonight.
For me this is the sweetest night.
You played with me all night last night.
Rub me again, my dear, as you did last night.

My love you take away all my pain.
At night you kiss me again and gain.
Oh my dear, rub me again tonight,
As you had done to me last night.

I never got so deep in love before.
Let me make love with you all night tonight.
Oh dear, your passion makes me love you more.
Rub me again tonight as you did last night.

GIVE ME A LITTLE KISS ON CHRISTMAS

I want you to give me a little kiss tonight.
I want a sweet kiss on Christmas.
I want a little kiss at midnight.
Give me a little sweet kiss on Christmas.

Your kiss awaked me tonight.
Now I am watching the snowflakes.
Your kiss awaked me tonight.
Now let's enjoy the snowflakes.

Darling, I want your kiss to make me glad.
Your love is not a fairy tale.
Your love, my dear, makes me glad.
Your love is not a fairy tale.

Oh my darling! Your are sweeter on Christmas.
You are sweeter than honeycomb tonight.
Oh darling! Here are my lips for one more kiss tonight.
I wish you a merry Christmas!